Copyright 2022 by Crystal Cox Shimer | instagram.com/CCShimer_UNC

Illustrated by Traci Champion | tracichampionphotos.com

All rights reserved. No portion of this book may be reproduced, stored in a retrieval system, or transmitted in any form or by any means—electronic, mechanical, photocopy, recording, scanning, or other—except for brief quotations for review or citing purposes, without the prior written permission of the author.

Published by Argyle Fox Publishing | argylefoxpublishing.com

ISBN 978-1-953259-30-1 (Paperback)

ISBN 978-1-953259-29-5 (Hardcover)

Pickles and Pork Rind are the best of friends who are very different, or so they're told.

Pickles wears bow ties
below his large ears,
has a long nose
and a voice full and bold.

Pork Rind wears a suit of armor, blue bandana, and little straw hat.

His tail is crooked, his legs are short, and he's shy when it's time to chat.

How these friends met is a long, funny tale that involved more than a little luck.

It happened on a wonderful, whimsical island known to the locals as Buck.

Pork Rind grew up on a country farm and was craving something more.

So they both left home and headed out,
following the island's tricky twists and bends.

Unsure just what they were looking for, they found each other and were instant best friends!

Ever since, they've been side by side,
ready with helping foot or snout—

whether Pork Rind needs a tall boost,

or Pickles can't get pickles out.

Together, these two have dived in oceans,

hiked up mountains,

camped in deserts,

and wished in fountains.

They've tried new foods,

bought hats with brims,

met new friends,

and gotten hairs trimmed.

Pickles and Pork Rind do so much together
it's hard for them to recall
the things that make them each so different.
Hmmm . . .
Maybe they're not so different after all!

CPSIA information can be obtained
at www.ICGtesting.com
Printed in the USA
BVHW020057060922
646291BV00003B/11